The Sensory System

Why am I ticklish?

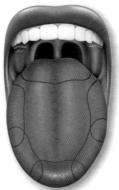

Sue Barraclough

Schools Library Service
Gwasaneth Llyfrgell Ysgolion

www.heinemannlibrary.co.uk

Visit our website to find out more information about Heinemann Library books.

To order:

☎ Phone 44 (0) 1865 888066

▤ Send a fax to 44 (0) 1865 314091

▢ Visit the Heinemann Bookshop at www.heinemannlibrary.co.uk to browse our catalogue and order online.

Heinemann Library is an imprint of Capstone Global Library Limited, a company incorporated in England and Wales having its registered office at 7 Pilgrim Street, London, EC4V 6LB – Registered company number: 6695582

Heinemann is a registered trademark of Pearson Education Limited, under licence to Capstone Global Library Limited

Text © Capstone Global Library Limited 2008
First published in hardback in 2008
Paperback edition first published in 2009

Editorial: Sarah Shannon, Sarah Chappelow and Rebecca Rissman
Design: Debbie Oatley and Steve Mead
Original illustrations © Capstone Global Library 2008
Illustrations: Tony Wilson
Picture research: Hannah Taylor and Maria Joannou
Production: Duncan Gilbert

Printed and bound in China by South China Printing Co. Ltd.

ISBN 978 0 431 13817 6 (hardback)
12 11 10 09 08
10 9 8 7 6 5 4 3 2 1

ISBN 978 0 431 13823 7 (paperback)
13 12 11 10 09
10 9 8 7 6 5 4 3 2 1

British Library Cataloguing in Publication Data

Barraclough, Sue
   The sensory system : why am I ticklish? - (Body systems)
   1. Senses and sensation - Juvenile literature 2. Nervous system - Juvenile literature
   I. Title
   612.8
A full catalogue record for this book is available from the British Library.

Acknowledgements

The publishers would like to thank the following for permission to reproduce photographs: © Alamy Images p.**8** (Momentum Creative Group); © Corbis pp.**5** (Chuck Savage), **10** (image100), **17** (Richard T. Nowitz), **28** (Take 2 Productions, Brand X); © Getty Images pp.**6**, **12** (PhotoDisc), **14**, **24** (Stone); © Pearson Education Ltd pp.**4** (Malcolm Harris), **19** (Tudor Photography); © Rex Features pp.**22** (Cosmo Condina, Stock Connection), **23** (Nils Jorgensen); © Science Photo Library pp.**20**, **26** (Omikron).

Cover photograph reproduced with permission of © Getty Images (Rubberball).

Every effort has been made to contact copyright holders of any material reproduced in this book. Any omissions will be rectified in subsequent printings if notice is given to the publishers.

Disclaimer

All Internet addresses (URLs) given in this book were valid at the time of going to press. However, due to the dynamic nature of the Internet, some addresses may have changed or ceased to exist since publication. While the author and the publishers regret any inconvenience this may cause readers, no responsibility for any such changes can be accepted by either the author or the publishers.

Contents

Some words are shown in bold, **like this**. You can find out what they mean by looking in the glossary.

What is my sensory system?

Your sensory system is the parts of your body that help you to understand the world around you. There are parts you can see, such as your nose and eyes. There are also parts inside your body that you cannot see, such as your **brain**.

You have five main senses. They are seeing, hearing, tasting, smelling, and touch. Your senses are involved in everything you do.

What do my eyes do?

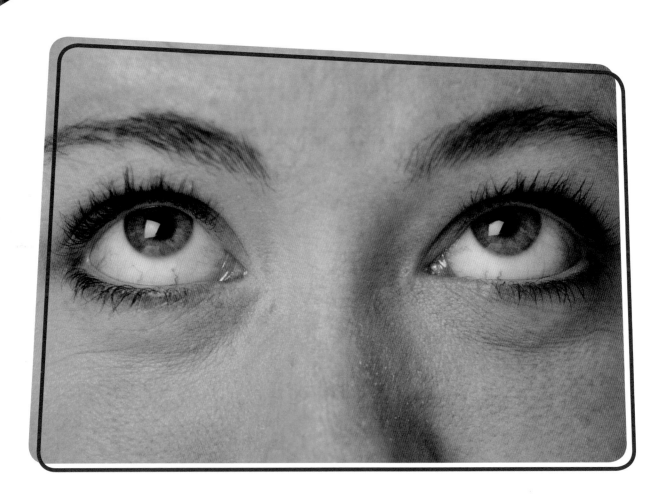

Your eyes are **organs** that help you to see. An organ is a part of your body that is made to do a certain job. Your eyes are in holes in your **skull** at the front of your head.

Your eyes are soft balls filled with a clear **jelly**. Your eyelids and eyelashes protect your eyes from dirt and sunshine. Blinking keeps your eyes wet and clean.

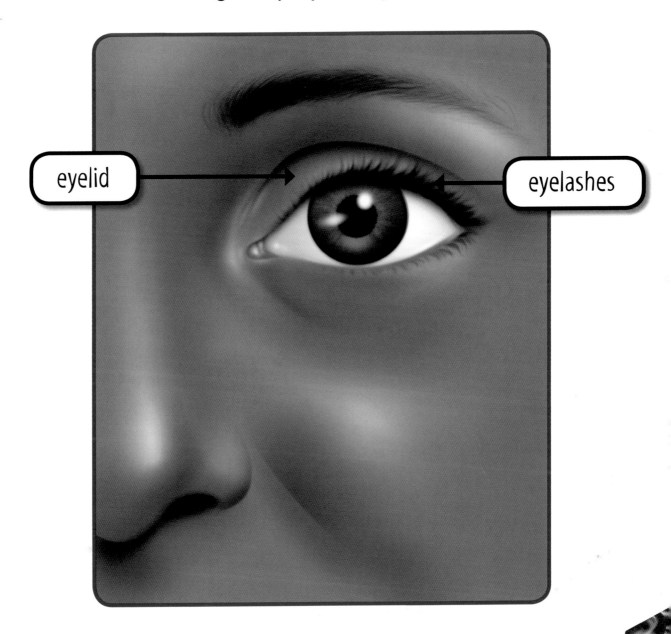

eyelid

eyelashes

How do eyes work?

Your eyes collect light that bounces off things around you. Light goes into the eyeball through the pupil. The pupil is the round black hole in the middle of your eye.

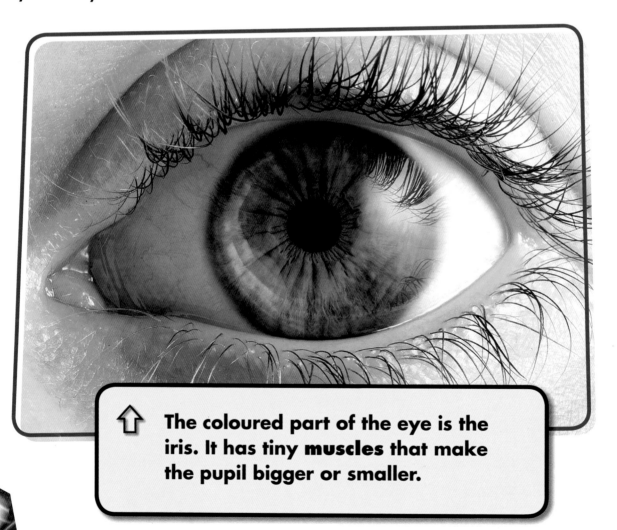

⇧ **The coloured part of the eye is the iris. It has tiny muscles that make the pupil bigger or smaller.**

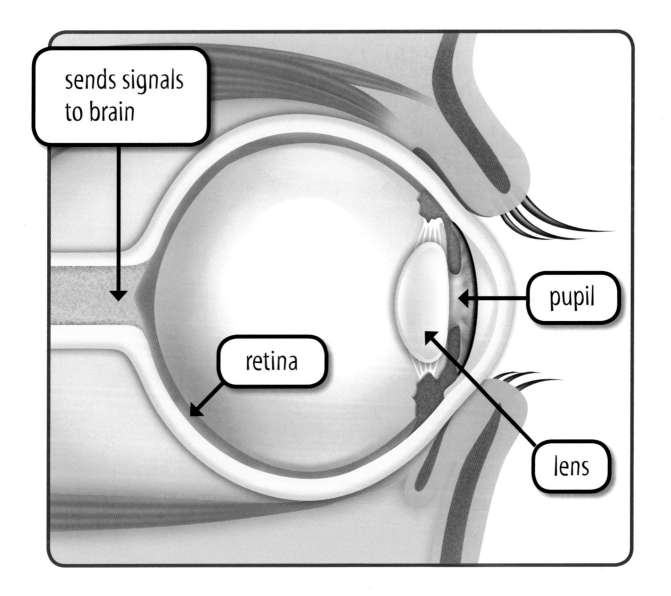

sends signals
to brain

pupil

retina

lens

A **lens** bends light onto the **retina**. The light makes a picture on the retina that is turned into **signals** to send to your **brain**. Your brain quickly sorts the signals so you see a picture of everything around you.

What do my ears do?

Your ears are **organs** that help you to hear. The outer part of your ear is made of a soft rubbery material. This material is called **cartilage**.

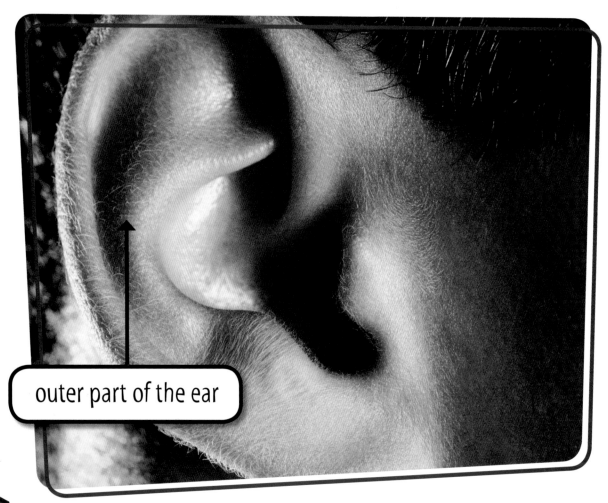

outer part of the ear

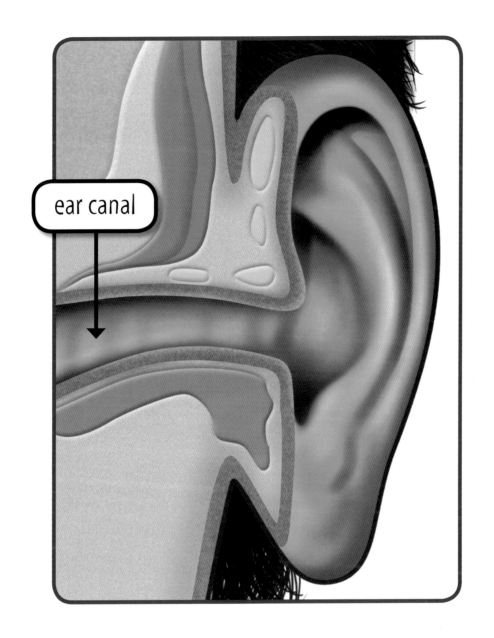

ear canal

The cartilage is shaped like a **funnel**. It is made to catch sounds and take them into a tunnel called the ear canal.

How do ears work?

Your ears work by collecting sounds. Sounds make movements in the air called sound waves. Sound waves travel into your ears through the ear canal.

The sound waves make your **eardrum** move. As your eardrum moves it moves three tiny bones in your ear. Inside your ear these movements are picked up and sent as **signals** to your **brain**.

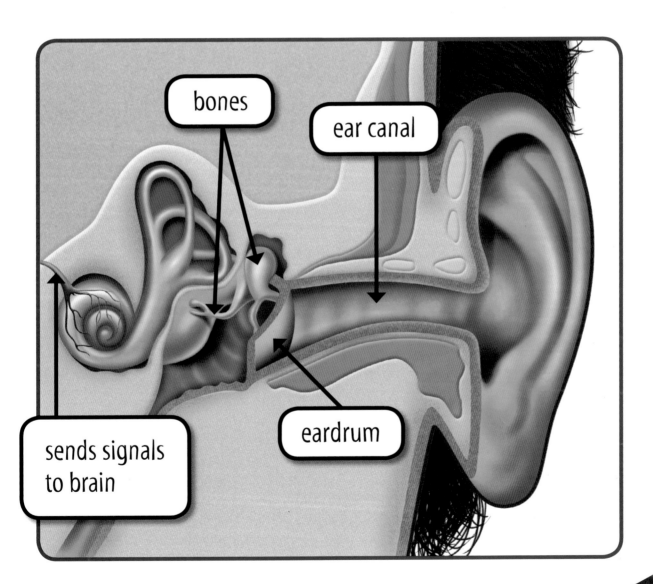

bones

ear canal

eardrum

sends signals to brain

What does my nose do?

Your nose is the part of your body that helps you to smell. It is made of bone, skin, and **cartilage**. It has two holes called nostrils.

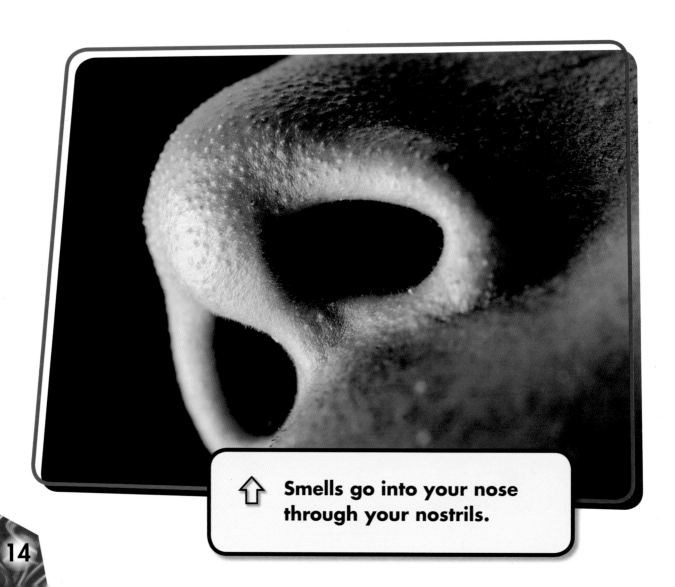

⬆ **Smells go into your nose through your nostrils.**

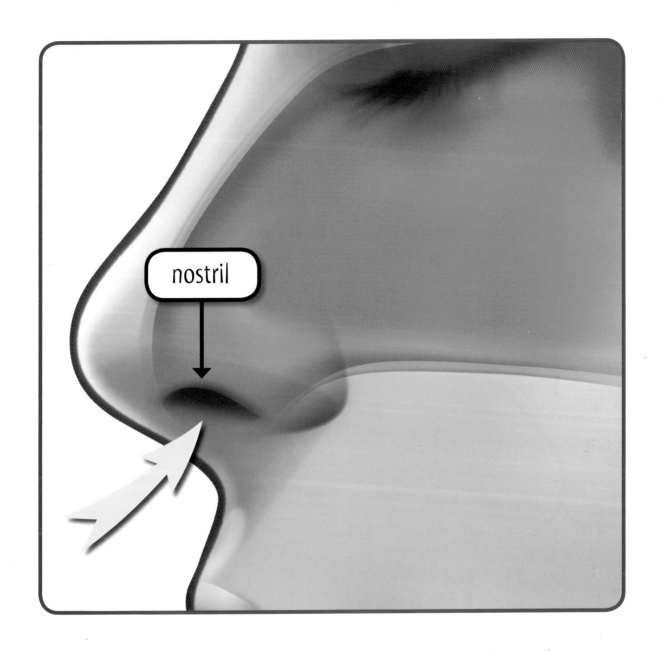

nostril

Your nose picks up different smells. Smelling things can keep you safe. A smell can tell you if food is rotten. The smell of smoke can warn you of a fire.

How do noses work?

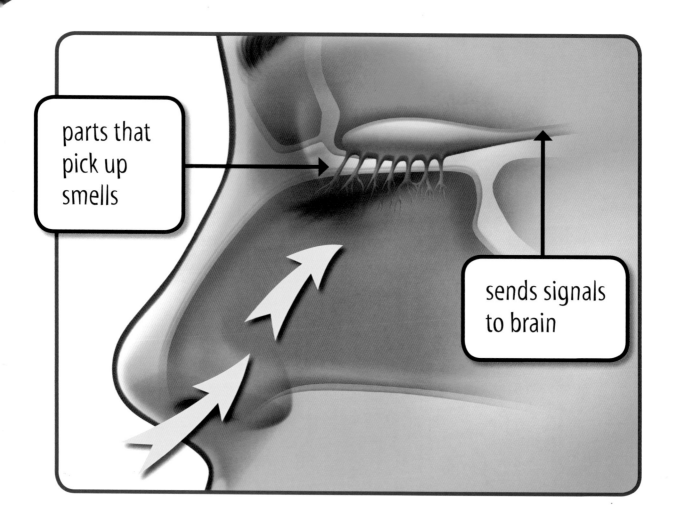

parts that pick up smells

sends signals to brain

Smells are carried in the air and go in to your nose as you breathe. There are tiny parts at the top of your nose that pick up smells.

Your nose sends **signals** about the smells to your brain. Your brain has lots of smells stored in your **memory**. Your **brain** can tell you what each smell is.

Blocking your nose can stop you from smelling things.

What does my tongue do?

Your tongue is a part of your mouth. You use your tongue to help chew and swallow food. You use your tongue to help make sounds when you speak.

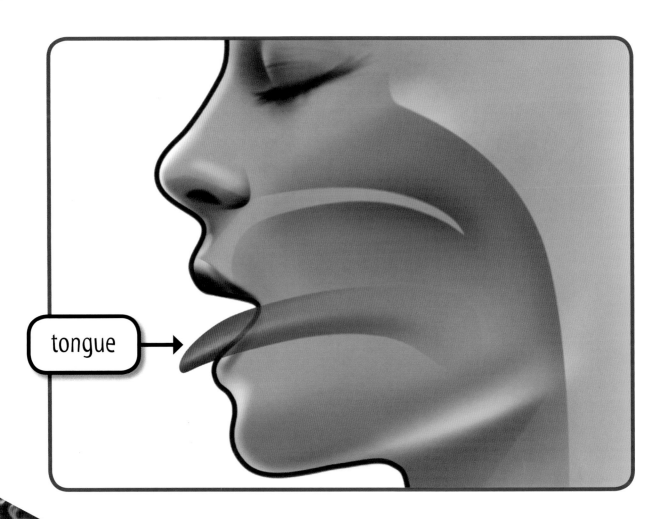

tongue

⇧ **Your senses of smell and taste work together. When your nose is blocked by a cold your sense of taste does not work very well.**

Your tongue helps you to taste and enjoy food. Your tongue also lets you know if something is not good to eat. Something that is bad to eat may taste bitter or horrible.

How does your tongue help you to taste?

⬆ **This is a magnified picture of the tongue. Taste buds are in the round, red circles.**

Your tongue is covered in tiny bumps called taste buds. Taste buds can sense five main tastes: salty, sweet, bitter, sour and umami. Umami is a meaty kind of taste.

Different parts of your tongue sense each type of taste. Your tongue sends **signals** to your **brain** about how something tastes.

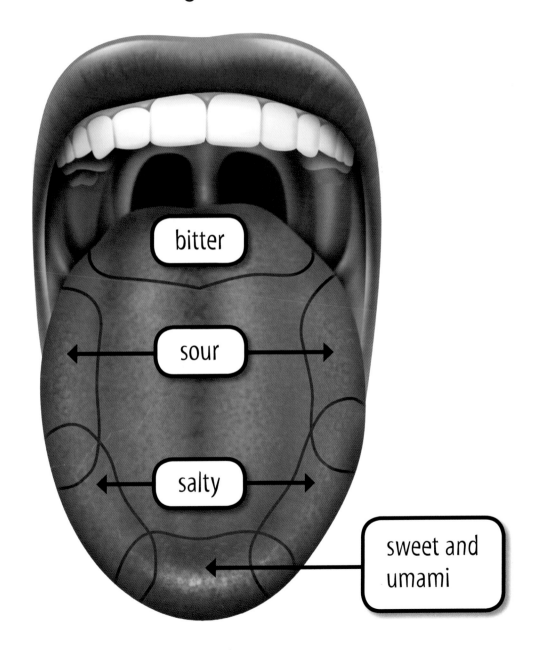

bitter

sour

salty

sweet and umami

What is my sense of touch?

Your sense of touch tells you what something feels like. It tells you if something is rough or smooth, or hot or cold.

You use your sense of touch to squeeze and shape things. ⇧

↑ **Touch warns you if something is sharp or prickly.**

Your sense of touch sends **signals** to the **brain**. This helps you to react to things. Touch tells you to scratch an itch on your leg. Touch helps you to move away from something that is prickly or hot.

How do I touch and feel?

Your feet can feel hard pebbles and cold water.

Signals about how things feel are sent to your **brain** along nerves. Nerves are like long, thin threads. They carry signals between your brain and parts of your body, such as your hands or feet.

At the end of each nerve is a nerve ending. Nerve endings send signals about how things feel to your brain. They tell your brain if something is hot, hard, painful, or soft. Your brain quickly tells your body how to react to each feeling.

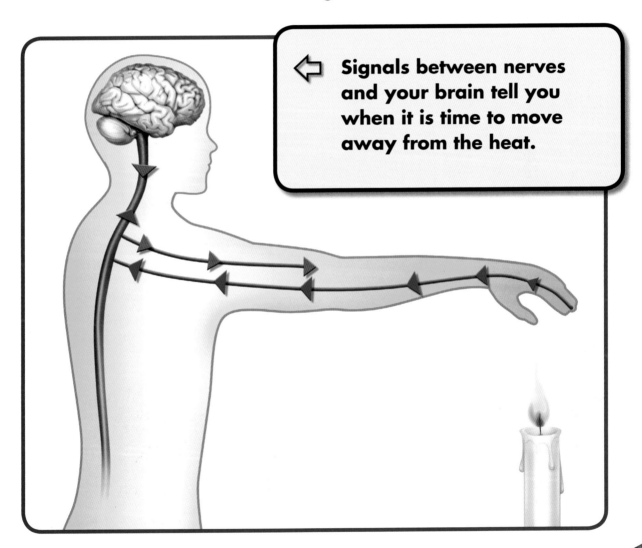

Signals between nerves and your brain tell you when it is time to move away from the heat.

The sensory system

Your **brain** is the most important part of your sensory system. Your brain is linked by nerves to your sensory **organs** and to all the nerve endings under your skin. Different parts of your brain work with each sense.

The part of your brain that works with your ears is shown here in red.

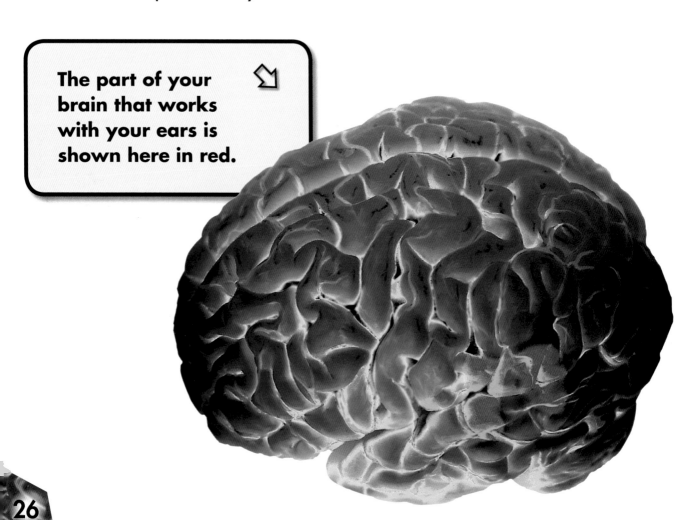

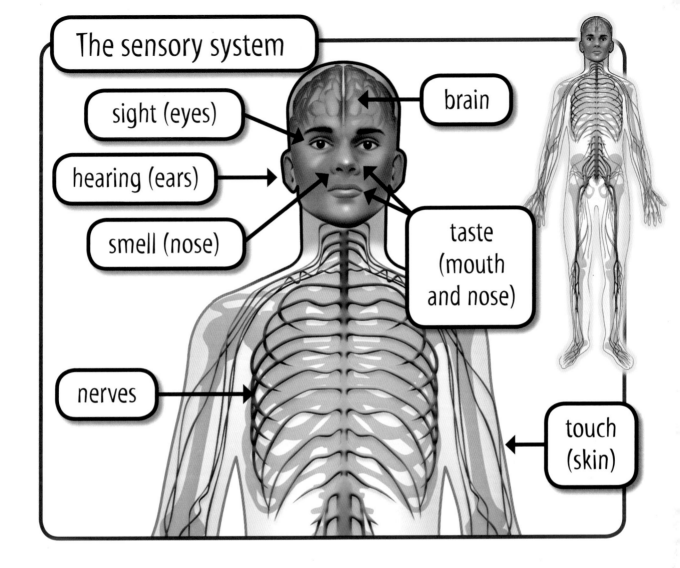

The sensory system

brain

sight (eyes)

hearing (ears)

smell (nose)

taste (mouth and nose)

nerves

touch (skin)

Your brain sorts and stores all the **signals** from your senses. Then it instantly sends millions of messages back to your body parts. Your brain tells all the different parts of your body what is happening and what to do.

Why am I ticklish?

You feel ticklish because of your sense of touch. A tickle is a light touch or a squeeze. Nerve endings pick up the feeling of the tickle and send a message to your **brain**.

Tickling often makes people laugh. Some people are more ticklish than others. Most people have one body part that is most ticklish.

Tickling can even be a little painful but it can still make us laugh! ⬇

Did you know?

In the dark your pupil gets bigger to let in more light. In bright light the pupil gets smaller to protect your eye.

Your sense of smell is linked to your **memory**. Certain smells will make you think of different places or people.

Your tongue is not good at sensing hot or cold. This is why it is easy to burn your tongue on hot food.

You have around 10,000 tiny taste buds in your mouth.

The most sensitive parts of your body are:
- lips and tongue
- face and neck
- fingertips and feet

Glossary

brain   organ inside your head that controls thinking, memory, feelings, and actions

cartilage   strong stretchy material that can be found in places such as your nose and ears

eardrum   thin piece of skin inside your ear. It moves backwards and forwards very quickly when sound waves hit it.

funnel   tube which is wide at the top and narrow at the bottom. It can be used for pouring liquids into bottles

jelly   soft, slightly wet substance

lens   part of your eye that helps you to see clearly

memory   power of your mind to remember things

muscle   stretchy part of your body that tightens and relaxes to make movement

organ   part of your body that has a certain job to do

retina   part at the back of your eye that is very sensitive to light

signal   message

skull   group of bones around your brain

Find out more

Books to read

Body in Action: Seeing by Claire Llewellyn (A&C Black, 2003)

Eyes and Ears by Simon Seymour (Harper Collins, 2003)

My Amazing Body: Senses by Angela Royston (Heinemann Library, 2005)

My Healthy Body: The Senses by Veronica Ross (Belitha Press, 2002)

Super Senses: Touching by Mary Mackill (Raintree, 2006). Other titles include Tasting, Smelling, and Special Animal Senses.

Websites

http://kidshealth.org/kid/body/tongue_SW.html
Find out about the tongue and how it helps you to taste. Choose "eye", "ear", or "nose" from the list to find out about how these body parts help you to sense things.

http://www.bbc.co.uk/science/humanbody/body/ factfiles/hearing/hearing_animation.shtml
This animation shows you how our sense of hearing works. Choose "sight", "smell" or "taste" from the list at the side to see animations about how these other senses work.

http://www.sciencemuseum.org.uk/on-line/brain/140.asp
Learn about your five senses and how they work together to give you information about the world.

Index